THE ALL SAINTS'

THE M

I am thrilled to support this new history of the Church I have been privileged to serve as Parish Priest for the past fourteen years.

All Saints is a sacred place. It oozes with holiness. I believe this is because the Living God has blessed it with His presence through many generations from Saxon times to our own. We can never know the names of all who worshipped God here but we thank him for them. They have given us a well built, well ordered and beautiful church.

The writer of Genesis tells us that Jacob had a vision of the angels of God ascending and descending on a special place and Jacob exclaimed,

> "How awesome is this place!
> This is none other than the house of God, and this is the gate of heaven." *(Genesis 28)*

Thomas Gray gives us his "Elegy written in a Country Churchyard" as a meditation on all those buried there,

> "let not Ambition mock their useful Toil, their homely Joys and Destiny obscure:" *(c.1760)*.

T.S.Eliot in his poem Little Gidding says,

> "you are here to kneel where prayer has been valid….And what the dead had no speech for, when living, They can tell you, being dead:….Here, the intersection of the timeless moment Is England and nowhere. Never and always."

Yes, we have a great deal to give thanks for and this splendid book is an expression of our thanks for our history. Congratulations to Geoffrey Robinson and the Banstead History Research Group who have helped us to appreciate our rich past so we may enjoy our vibrant present and hand on to the future the fruits of our labours.

DAVID CHANCE, *Vicar of Banstead. April 2007*

© April 2007 Banstead History Research Group.
All Rights Reserved.

No reproduction permitted by any means without the express
permission in writing of the Publishers:
Banstead History Research Group

A catalogue record for this book is available from the British Library
ISBN 978-0-9550768-3-1

Front cover: The church from the west. *(February 2007)*
Inside front cover: The nave leading to the chancel. *(February 2007)*
Inside back cover: The nave from the chancel. *(August 2006)*
Back cover: The church from the north. *(August 2006)*

Printed by Print Solutions Partnership, 55 Sandy Lane South, Wallington, Surrey SM6 9RQ
Tel: 020 8404 3922   email: print@pspartnership.co.uk

Introduction

Banstead Village is so called nowadays to distinguish it from other parts of the district that have come into existence since large scale building development began in the 1920s.

The days of Banstead as a village are gone but reminders of its distant past are still to be found. Foremost among these is the parish church of All Saints, a Grade II Listed building. This has for centuries played an important part in the life of Banstead and will continue to do so for as long as we can foresee.

This book is not a guide to the church. It is however, intended as a contribution to our knowledge of its history in the absence of anything better currently available. The church has a number of unusual features that are not widely known and may be of interest to the general public, even if they do not go there regularly. My own interest arises from a long familiarity with the church and its surroundings. Both my parents are buried in the churchyard and I expect to join them there in the fullness of time.

This general history of the church is followed by a record of the important manor house which used to stand to the south-east of the church in the 13th and 14th centuries. A list, as far as is known, of the vicars who have served the church over its long history is also supplied.

Those interested in learning more about the interior of the church should consult the Victoria County History of Surrey. Although published a hundred years ago it is only partly out of date. It does however, describe the chief features of the church at that time.

I am much indebted to Ralph Maciejewski for his help in producing this book and the many present day photographs, and to John Sweetman, author of the admirable two volume History of Banstead published in 2005, for his advice generally.

And lastly my thanks to the vicar, the Rev. David Chance, for his helpful suggestions, his drawing of the church and for kindly supplying the foreword.

Geoffrey Robinson
Banstead,
April 2007

The south porch of the church *(March 2007)*

Contents

The church, its history and surroundings 1
    Environs of the church 1
    Earliest church 2
    Churchyard mound 3
    Old yew tree 3
    Site of church 5
    Early church building 6
    Church at Banstead 6
    Size of church 7
    Entrance to church 7
    Church and manor 7
    Church and clergy 8
    Hubert de Burgh 13
    Tower 13
    Place of sanctuary 13
    First known ordination 15
    Dissolution of Priory 15
    Advowson 15
    Parish records 16
    Effect of Civil War 16
    Unwelcome changes 21
    Post-Restoration 21
    Censuses 21
    Vicarage 22
    Vicar and neighbour 23
    15th-18th century 23
    The steeple 24
    19th century 29
    The church pre-"restoration" 29
    Paintings by Yates 29
    Reredos 30
    Paintings by Hassell 30
    Font 35
    Seating 35
    Oldest part of church 35
    Consecration cross 36
    Church music 36

Church organ 36
The restoration in the 1860s 37
The Rossetti window 37
Effect of restoration 38
Other changes to interior 39
Memorials 39
Windows 39
Renewal of roof 40
Church bells 40
Bellringing 45
Church clock 46
Twentieth century 46
Church Institute 51
Banstead Five Churches 51
Churchyard 51
War memorial 52
Garton Memorial Chapel 52

THE HISTORY OF THE MANOR HOUSE 54
Twentieth century 54
Royal Banstead 55
The extent of the manor house 56
Building work 56
Further work in 1363 57
The excavations in 1973 57

THE KNOWN VICARS OF ALL SAINTS' BANSTEAD 60

MAIN SOURCES 62

INDEX 63

The Church, its History and Surroundings

All Saints Church, Banstead — David Chance

Figure 1. The church clock.
Installed in 1931 with funds provided by Colonel T. F. Parkinson, a bellringer, in memory of his son.

The Church, its History and Surroundings

The parish church of Banstead is by far the oldest building in the district. Situated just off the High Street, it is likely that the surrounding area was the earliest inhabited place in Banstead, and that there has been a church on the site for at least 1,000 years.

Although this is not apparent nowadays, it is a local high point, being about 526 feet (160 metres) above sea level. A tourist guide of 1887 stated that the church stood on very high ground, and with its lofty spire was a conspicuous feature in the landscape, giving fine views from the churchyard. Together with Leith Hill and Bagshot Heath the site formed one of the three original Ordnance Survey triangulation stations for Surrey. The OS benchmark survives outside the bottom of the west window of the church.

Before the area around it was built up, there were commanding views all round, particularly to the north, where the bare grassy slopes of the North Downs gradually give way to the more fertile soil of Banstead. The several ponds in the sand, gravel and clay soil there all contributed to make it a natural choice for settlement by early man.

At the time of the Domesday Survey of 1086, Banstead was recorded as having an adult male population of 28 villagers, 15 cottagers and 7 serfs, indicating a total community of perhaps 200 men, women and children. There was also a church, probably on the site of the present one.

Environs of the church

A former mound south of the church, once surmounted by an old yew tree, was probably a barrow of pre-Christian origin. It seems likely that the whole area was a burial ground and a place for worship and community activity even before Christianity came to Surrey in the 7th century. It was the policy of the early missionaries not to destroy places of pagan worship, but to sanctify and absorb them into the Christian church.

This ensured that the powerful religious associations of a site were sustained, and continuity of worship guaranteed. The surroundings were then converted to a place of Christian worship by the setting up of an altar. Burials would have continued to take place in the vicinity, and later a chapel built to protect the altar and offer the priest and congregation some shelter from the elements.

EARLIEST CHURCH

It is not at all unusual for a parish churchyard to be older than the nearby church, and that appears to be the case in Banstead. When a chapel came to be built, it was the practice for it to be set up on the northern side of the enclosure so that its shadow did not fall on the graves. Consequently the dead were normally buried on the south side of the church.

The first church would have been timber-framed, with walls of wattle and daub, as most parish churches and even cathedrals were at that time. The nearest available building stone was firestone, mined from quarries in the Reigate area. This was found to have been used for the foundations of the nearby 13th century manor house, and again when the church was rebuilt in its present more solid form. However, although easily worked and very suitable for internal use, its absorbent character made it vulnerable to frost and it needed, as here, to be faced with flint if used on exterior surfaces.

The authoritative Victoria County History of Surrey, published a hundred years ago, declared the church to have been over-restored but still of very great interest.

The nave, it observes, probably retains the plan of a building considerably earlier than any detail now existing, the great height and comparative thinness of the walls of the nave suggesting a possible pre-Conquest origin. The walls of the nave are about 24 feet (7.3m) high, where 18 feet (5.5m) would have been the normal height of a Norman building. They are about 16 feet (5.1m) wide.

Figure 2. The stone in All Saints churchyard marks the reburied remains of the Anglo Saxon Christians who were discovered at a site off Merland Rise, Banstead in 1986.

CHURCHYARD MOUND

As already mentioned, there can be discerned in the churchyard immediately south of the church what had once been a grassy knoll. This mound originally had the appearance of a pre-Christian burial mound similar to Tumble Beacon, the Scheduled Ancient Monument in The Drive, about a mile away, thought to be of Bronze Age origin.

As the mound is in consecrated ground it is unlikely to be possible to establish whether it was indeed a pre-Christian tumulus, but there is evidence of very early settlement in the locality, both Christian and pre-Christian. Some 35 graves dating from the 7th century, discovered in 1986 at a site off Merland Rise, about two miles away, were found to contain burials in shrouds in orderly rows on an east-west axis, indicating Christian burial. They were later reburied in Banstead churchyard, not far from the supposed tumulus.

OLD YEW TREE

The churchyard mound was once surmounted by a notable old yew tree *(see figure 4)* which unfortunately died after being vandalised some 30 or so years ago. A much younger yew tree survives nearby.

Dating yew trees is always difficult but the one at Banstead was certainly very old. In a survey made in 1880 of yew trees in Surrey churchyards its girth five feet above ground level was put at 15 feet 3 inches (about 4.65 metres) and its age at 900 years, suggesting that it was planted about the year 1000. It is thought that it may have marked the spot where a portable wooden altar would have been used by missionary priests before the first church was built there.

In England the clergy are thought to have planted churchyard yews as they had in Normandy before the Conquest. This originally arose from a pre-Christian belief in the power of the tree to ward off evil spirits. The practice was continued in newly consecrated churchyards to provide evergreen foliage for the nearby church at Easter and other festivals.

It may be relevant that King Edward I, who in 1273 became lord of the manor of Banstead which included the church, and who is known to have visited his very exposed manor house several times in 1305 and earlier, decreed in 1307 that yew trees be planted to protect churches from high winds and storms. This was usually done on the south side to protect the doorway, as would have been the case here.

Figure 3. The yew planted in the churchyard by the Conservation Foundation for the third Christian Millennium.

Figure 4. *The old yew tree in All Saints churchyard in 1910. It's girth was measured in 1880 as 15 feet 3 inches (4.65 metres) at five feet above ground making it around 900 years old.*

SITE OF CHURCH

At some time during the reign of Henry I (1100-1135) Tirel de Maniers, the patron of the living with the advowson, or right of nomination to a benefice, gave the church and other property to the Priory of St Mary Overy, which was on the site of the present-day Southwark Cathedral.

Some years later, believed to be in 1170, his grandson Nigel de Mowbray, the new patron and lord of the manor, confirmed the grant and himself made a gift to the Priory of certain property. This gift, made before the earliest date currently assigned to any part of the church as it is now, included:-

"......the orchard which is on the north between the church of Benested and the road which goes to the house of Vitalis of Sutton, and between the road which leads to my court house and the path which on the west leads to the church."

The "road which goes to the house of Vitalis of Sutton", a signatory to the deed, is thought to be the High Street, known to have existed in 1433 and which probably dates from much earlier. The court or manor house was to the south-east of the church and with the path on the west leading to the church it is clear that the orchard of 1170 was much the same piece of land between the church and the High Street as an area there conveyed to the church in 1904.

This land is still known as "the orchard", more than 800 years later, despite the apparent absence over the years of any indication as to the type of fruit tree there. The inference therefore is that the present church is on the site of the earlier church, especially as foundations of a wall are said to have been uncovered when the church floor was retiled some 25 years ago.

Nigellus de Moubrai omnibus hominibus suis francis et anglis et universis Sancte Matris ecclesie filiis tam presentibus quam futuris; salutem. Notum sit omnibus vobis me concessisse et de-disse et hac mea carta confirmasse deo et beate Marie et Canonicis ecclesie sancte Marie de Sudwurch' in liberam et perpetuam elemosinam pomerium quod est apud aquilonem inter ecclesiam de Benested et viam que graditur apud domum Vitalis de Sutt' et inter viam que ducit ad curiam meam et semitam que in occidente ducit ad Ecclesiam.

Figure 5. The original text highlighted with the Latin text below, of the grant by Nigel de Mowbray of an Orchard to the Canons of St. Mary Overie, Southwark. *(Approx. 1170 AD.).*

Figure 6. The view of the church from the north. *(Seago 1724)*

The site of the church and the oldest part of the churchyard are again recorded as having been given to the Priory in 1192 by the lord of the manor Nigel de Mowbray, evidently confirming the earlier grant. The monastery would then have appointed a priest to represent it, known as the vicar, as the Prior is known to have done in 1325.

EARLY CHURCH BUILDING

After the energetic new parish church building that took place immediately after the Norman Conquest, most of church construction work was in adding to the fabric of existing buildings. Since daily services needed to be carried on without interruption while work was in progress, the new building work would have been done around and above the existing building. The nave and chancel would have been left as undisturbed as possible until all was finished.

The existing side walls and roof would then have been pulled down and the debris removed through a temporary archway knocked through one of the walls for the purpose. Although no evidence of this survives at Banstead, such a piecemeal method is assumed to be one reason why the walls of the chancel are not in line or square with the nave.

CHURCH AT BANSTEAD

Banstead church may not have been built as an entity but it is remarkable because of the early date by which it evidently developed as a very complete church. From earliest times it seems to have had a nave with north and south aisles and a chancel with north and south chapels. If it was indeed built in a single period and in pursuit of a single plan, it would, in the view of J. E. Morris, be one of the most remarkable churches in Surrey (see plan).

The stonework of the nave arcades shows distinctive tooling dated by an authority as circa 1180 and the chancel, north chapel and tower is dated at some 10 to 40 years later. If correct, it means that large scale building work must have taken place in this quite short period.

So large was the church that despite the growth over the years of the village and its population and consequent congregations, no further increase in its size has been needed. Its "footprint" remained the same until 1820, some 600 years or so later, and then it was only changed to add a vestry room at the western end to provide better accommodation for the parish meetings.

SIZE OF CHURCH

The church was a large and handsome building for what was then a small and unimportant hamlet in an area of comparatively poor soil and sparse population. One must wonder how this came about, bearing in mind the short period of building involved and the absence of a local building stone.

Monasteries were not always zealous in church-building and the most likely explanation here is that the driving force was the lord of the manor. From 1217 to 1243 this was the formidable and influential Hubert de Burgh, of whom more later.

ENTRANCE TO CHURCH

Most early churches had north and south entrances, some a west one as well. A painting of Banstead church in 1826 by Gideon Yates shows a large Early English period (c.1150 to 1270) doorway into the tower from the west, evidently removed in the "restoration" of the 1860s. Its size suggests that it was originally the main entrance to the church via the tower *(see figure 9)*.

The western entrance to a church was originally a feature in Saxon times but after the Norman Conquest it tended to be rarely used except for ceremonial occasions such as the annual procession on Palm Sunday. Sometimes the church was built first and then a tower added to cover the entrance, but at Banstead the tower is so massive that it may well have had another purpose.

CHURCH AND MANOR

In general it was the south door that was the main door to a church and this seems to have been the case at Banstead, where it originally opened out on to the manor house. The present south porch is not particularly old, having been rebuilt in the 1860s, but it is still more substantial than the north porch, also rebuilt at that time.

In 1275 the manor of Banstead had passed to the Crown, and it was a royal manor until 1376. Royalty stayed there several times during that period and as a result some documentary and other evidence about the manor house and its surroundings has survived. This is detailed later in this book. It shows the lord's residence to have been a rambling collection of buildings to the south and east of the church. Despite being the most important house in the village the manor house at that time was mainly timber-framed with walls of wattle and daub, like the rest of the village.

The only stone used in it would have been for fireplaces and an undercroft, remains of which have since been uncovered. No other building as solidly based as the church is thought to have been built in Banstead until some 400 years later when brick or stone and flint began to supersede timber as the local building material.

In 1376 the manor house ceased to be a royal residence and it gradually fell into disuse and decay. As the village grew and the High Street became more important, the north door of the church evidently took over as the main entrance. This door was renewed in the 15th century when the north aisle was widened and the north wall rebuilt in line with the wall of the north chapel.

CHURCH AND CLERGY

In medieval times the church porch was important as the centre of parish life and a public meeting place. It was the place for the publication of marriage banns and the first part of the marriage service and where a baby taken for baptism was received by the priest for the first part of the service. The coroner sat here and it was considered the proper place for much civil business such as the signing of public documents.

The church and religious observance played a crucial role in the local community, permeating all aspects of daily experience. Most people attended to see and hear the priest celebrate a daily Mass and the more pious were present also at Mattins and Evensong on Sunday. Most preaching was done outside the church in the churchyard but the priest was still required to be in church many times a day.

This might have been difficult for the early clergy, who may well have been little better educated than their congregation. Very few of their flock would have understood a word of the Latin of the services. There was no seating in the churches nor a pulpit for the vicar.

Very few vicars possessed a Bible and the preaching of a sermon would have been quite a rare event. However this changed following the printing of the Bible in English in 1538, and a hundred years later nearly all the clergy beneficed in Surrey were said to be graduates.

Figure 7. The view of the church from the east. *(General Sir Charles Ellicombe 1848).*
Reproduced by permission of London Borough of Lambeth, Archives Department.

Figure 8. The view of the church from the east *(1936).*

Figure 9. The view of the church from the west. *(Gideon Yates 1826)*
Reproduced by permission of London Borough of Lambeth, Archives Department.

Figure 10. The view of the church from the west. *(August 2006)*

Figure 11. View from the south of the Vicarage with the church to the right. *(Edward Hassell 1826)*
Reproduced by kind permission of Michael Lambert.

Figure 12. View of the Vicarage from the north. *(Edward Hassell 1826)*
Reproduced by kind permission of Michael Lambert.

Hubert de Burgh

After the death of Nigel de Mowbray about 1192 the manor of Banstead passed to his son William. He was one of the barons who opposed King John and was one of the 25 executors of the Magna Carta in 1215. In 1217 the manor was acquired by Hubert de Burgh, who had recently been Sheriff of Surrey and, one of the king's closest advisers, had also been an executor of the Magna Carta at Runnymede, but on the other side.

For the next 20 years or so Hubert was Justiciar or Chief Justice, the highest possible office under the King, and thus one of the most powerful men in the land. His impact on Banstead was such that even five hundred years later, in 1728, it was said of de Burgh that the local people "seem to retain the remembrance of him to this day". After his death the manor passed to his son and then in 1273 to the Crown.

The known dating, and the scale of the work done to the church, suggests that it was put in hand during the years 1217-1243 when Hubert de Burgh held the manor. He is known to have performed generously the acts of piety expected of an influential layman at that time.

Tower

The immensely thick and strong church tower is of interest, the west wall being 6ft 5in (nearly 2 metres) thick. Dated by one authority at about 1190-1220 it has been said that the walls were doubtless intended to be carried up to a greater height than they are now. However there must be the possibility that the great thickness of the walls was for defensive purposes rather than to take a higher steeple. The corners are supported by angle buttresses typical of the 13th century.

Church towers had their origin in military defence, the term "belfry" being of Teutonic origin and meaning "a defensive place of shelter". Later it came to mean a watch tower or alarm bell tower and in places massive square towers provided refuges for the whole community.

It may be significant that Hubert de Burgh had in 1201 been granted the lordship of three castles in the Welsh Marches, where frequent raids and border disputes were a way of life. In one of them, Skenfrith, he built a massive castle and very probably the nearby church also. This has walls five feet thick and a "dovecote" capping the tower where stores could be housed and which could be made into a partial fortress in times of danger *(see figure 13)*.

Place of Sanctuary

In an eventful life Hubert de Burgh made many enemies, and eventually fell from power in 1232. In his lifetime he had twice sought sanctuary in churches, knowing that a fugitive was safe once he reached consecrated ground. The great strength of the tower at Banstead may well be connected with his time as lord of the manor here.

As well as their use in military defence, church towers were often used as lookouts and guides for travellers. Later their main function was as belfries to support the church bells. Bells were important in village life, not only for calling people to church and celebrate occasions such as weddings, but also to mark the divisions of the day before clocks came into common use.

Louvred boards in the window in the top part of the tower to allow out the sound of the bells are shown in the earliest illustrations of All Saints and have probably been there since very early times. Obviously the more bells there are and the higher they are hung, the further they can be heard and the more important is the church.

Figure 13. Skenfrith Church tower.

It is not known when the Banstead church steeple was first erected above the tower. It may perhaps have replaced a "dovecote" capping such as that at Skenfrith mentioned earlier. An inventory of the church in 1549 at the time of the Reformation showed that its steeple contained five bells, at a time when most comparable churches had only two or three.

Figure 14. View from the north of the church in the 18th century.

They were all removed for sale or melting down in 1553 and the oldest bell today is dated 1585. John Aubrey, writing between 1673-92, reported that the church at that time had six bells, showing that five more must have been added in the previous hundred years.

FIRST KNOWN ORDINATION

The first known reference to the ordination of a vicar is on May 7 th 1316 when Nicholas de Habbourne was ordained, succeeding one Ranulph who retired "labouring under great infirmity of body and an incurable disorder". The names of most of the incumbents since then are known (see Appendix). The first record of the church having been dedicated to All Saints appears in the Bishop's Register at the time of the institution of John Sydenhale as vicar on 12th January 1389.

DISSOLUTION OF PRIORY

In 1534 the reformed Church of England was established with Henry VIII as its titular head and Papal jurisdiction was renounced. This was followed in 1537-9 by the dissolution of Southwark Priory and other monasteries, breaking the connection between the Priory and the local church.

In 1549 three Commissioners appointed by advisers to Henry's son, the 12 year old Edward VI, visited the church and made an inventory of its goods and ornaments. This included the five steeple bells, a silver chalice weighing 14 ounces, two candlesticks for the altar, brass goods weighing 16 lbs and a large number of altar cloths, surplices and other vestments.

Four years later in 1553 all the goods, ornaments and vestments were taken "for the King's use" and sold or melted down except for the chalice and a green cope left for the communion table. A chalice for the consecrated wine had been bequeathed to the church by the vicar John Woodcrofte in 1485 but the silver chalice of 1549 was more likely one left to the church by a later vicar, William Cutson, in 1537 together with a pax of silver and a pair of cruets.

ADVOWSON

After the Dissolution the advowson, or right of appointing the priest to the parish, was given to Robert Moys and later passed to his grandson John and then to John's widow Frances (née Buckle). The Moys family lived at the large rectory known as Canons near Burgh Heath. Centuries earlier in 1318 a licence had been granted to Juliana, widow of Robert de Walton, for an oratory or portable altar at Canons. Thomas de Banstede was ordained there, first as a deacon and then as the priest.

From Frances Moys the advowson passed in 1663 to her brother Christopher (later Sir Christopher) Buckle, whose family unobtrusively exercised the right until 1816. In that year Christopher Buckle of Nork House, the sixth and last of that name, died. The succession then passed to a cousin the Reverend William Buckle of Pyrton, Oxfordshire who, after the death of the incumbent in Banstead in 1822, took up the living there.

He was succeeded in 1832 by his elder son, the Reverend William Lewis Buckle, who in 1846 conveyed the advowson and his large estate of Nork, valued at £60,000, to the sixth Earl of Egmont. The Earl's descendants retained it until its transfer to the See of Guildford in 1929, following the death of the ninth Earl, so that the Bishop of Guildford is now the patron of the living.

PARISH RECORDS

In 1538 parishes were required to keep registers of births, marriages and deaths. The earliest registers for Banstead have survived and transcripts of the first two books were made and published in 1896. The first register, entitled "the Weddyng, the Chrystenyng and the Beryying Booke off Bansteyde", with entries from 1547 to 1618, is in poor condition with the writing faded and sometimes illegible. The second volume records baptisms from 1620 to 1783, marriages from 1616 to 1753 and burials from 1617 to 1789.

The entries in them are often carelessly made, possibly by an underling. The original entry has often been corrected or added to in another hand, perhaps the vicar's, and some of the pages are missing or torn. This particularly applies to the registers from 1642 to the Restoration where entries are erratic with large variations in the number of births, marriages and burials recorded each year and no burials at all shown for some years. These archives are now kept at the Surrey History Centre in Woking.

EFFECT OF CIVIL WAR

It is not known who was vicar of Banstead at the time of the Civil War from 1642-1649 but it must have been a difficult time for him. Instructions had been issued in 1631 that the Royal Arms were to be painted or repaired in all churches, with the Ten Commandments, and it is known that during the Commonwealth many examples of the Royal Arms were destroyed, hidden or defaced.

There exists on a wall in Well Farm, Banstead some wooden panelling, the top half of which contains a large rather crudely painted Stuart coat of arms over which is writtten "FEAR GOD AND HONOUR THE KING". It has been suggested that this had been removed for safety from All Saints Church during the Civil War and this may well be so, although there is no supporting evidence.

In 1645 an ordinance was passed forbidding the use of the Book of Common Prayer and prescribing new liturgical forms considered more suitable, affecting both the layout of the church and the conduct of services. These new rules were very much at variance with long accepted practice and subjected the Church to many unwelcome restrictions.

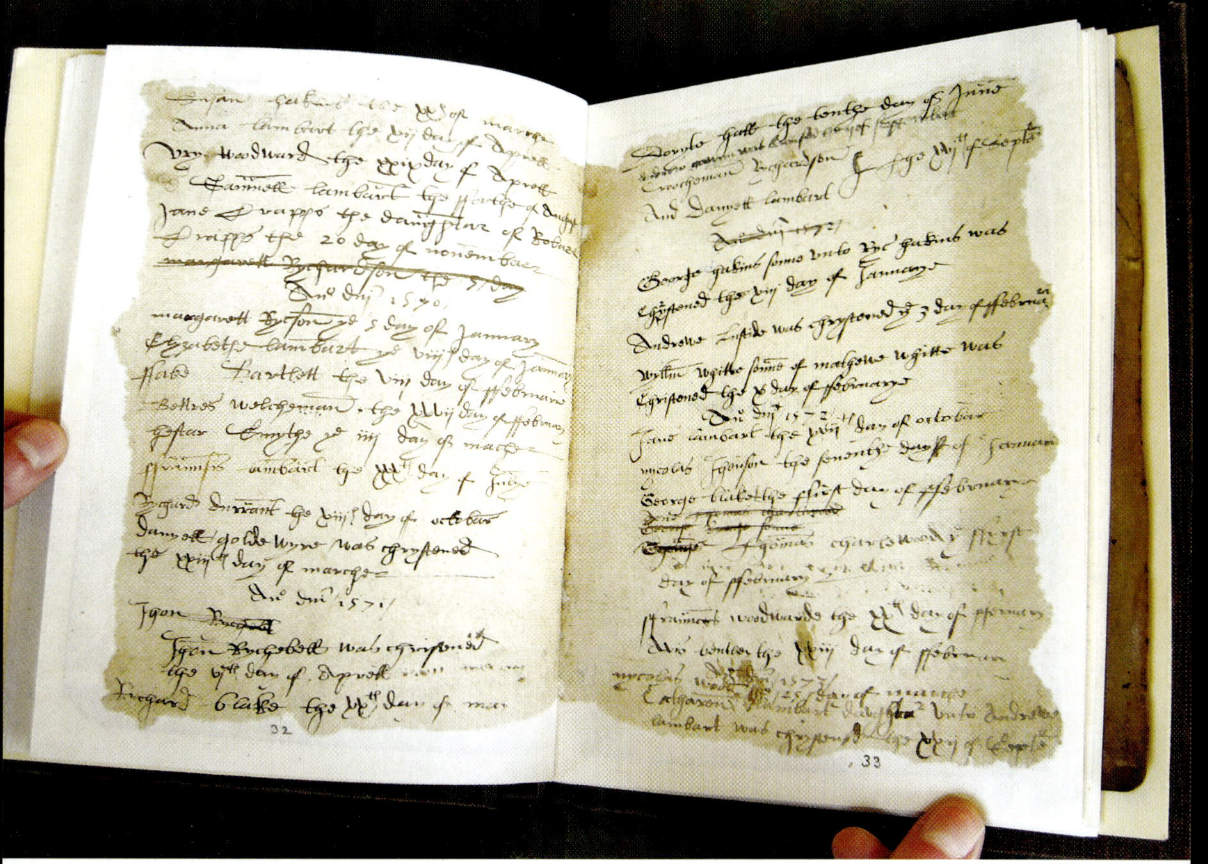

Figure 15. Pages from the second volume of the parish register of Banstead. *Reproduced by kind permission of the Surrey History Centre.*

Figure 16. The Banstead Psalm from the "The Compleat Book of Psalmody". *(James Evision, London 1751).*

Figure 17. View from the north east of the church before the restoration in the 1860s.

Figure 18. View from the north east of the church. *(August 2006)*

Figure 19. View of the church from the east. *(Gideon Yates 1826)*
Reproduced by permission of London Borough of Lambeth, Archives Department.

Figure 20. View of the church from the south. *(Edward Hassell 1830)*
Reproduced by kind permission of Michael Lambert.

Unwelcome Changes

Thus from 1653 onwards an Act removed the recording of births and burials into the hands of a civilian appointed for the purpose and substituted a form of marriage before a Justice of the Peace for marriage in church. No other form of marriage was permitted by law.

The changes seem to have been reluctantly accepted but the parish registers show that baptisms, burials and marriages continued to take place in church, the marriages being additional to the civil marriage ceremony. All the new rules had gone by the time of the Restoration in 1660.

In 1651 James Staynes had been appointed as vicar. He seems to have complied with the new regime sufficiently to retain office and keep the church going. The records also show him as having been admitted on the presentation of Richard Cromwell, Lord Protector of the Commonwealth, in October 1658. He died in March 1659, to be succeeded later in the year by the Rev Samuel Hinde.

Post-Restoration

In 1660 following the Restoration a statute renewed the requirement for the Royal Coat of Arms to be displayed in all churches. In 1669 two impressive copies of the Charles II Revised Book of Common Prayer and bearing the Buckle coat of arms were presented to the church by Sir Christopher Buckle, not long after he had become patron and holder of the advowson. A new Book of Common Prayer was bought for the church in 1716 at the same time that painting a new Royal Coat of Arms and other work was undertaken.

Censuses

In 1725 at the Bishop's Visitation the vicar, John Edwards, estimated the population of the parish at about 400, with on average about 5 marriages, 12 births and 8 deaths a year. There was not one "Papist" that he knew of, but there were a man and his wife who were Anabaptists and one woman Presbyterian.

At a later Bishop's Visitation in 1788 the then vicar estimated the parish population at about 600-700 with on average about 3 marriages, 21 births and 13 burials a year. There were no Papists or Protestant dissenters that he knew of. In 1801 the first official Census showed a population of 717 persons in the 140 inhabited houses, a figure that by 1831 had risen to 991.

On 30th March 1851 a Census of Religious Worship in Britain was held in conjunction with the Population Census for that year. These showed Banstead to have a total population of 1,270 and the church to have 260 seats. On Census Day there were 103 attending in the morning and 118 in the afternoon, plus 46 Sunday School children in the morning and 47 in the afternoon. The results of this census, the first of its kind, were in general a disappointment to the clergy and it was not repeated.

Figure 21. View of the church from the north east before the restoration in the 1860s. *(Cracklow). (Copyright of Surrey History Service).*

Vicarage

The first record of a local vicarage is in 1291 when it was valued at 6 marcs and 20 pence (1 marc was equal to two thirds of a pound). This compares with the 20 marcs valuation of the church itself and is consistent with a working rule that the vicarage valuation should be about one third that of the church, it being difficult to estimate precisely the value of tithes and offerings to the vicar.

In 1535 the vicarage had a small orchard, a garden and one acre of glebe land. The site of the first vicarage is not known for certain but was probably the same as the later vicarage. For some 300 years from the 17th century onwards this was about 50 yards north-west of the church and accessed from the roadway leading from the High Street to the church.

The vicarage garden at the beginning of the 18th century was commented on by the diarist Celia Fiennes and other visitors. The vicar, Nathaniel Hinde, was well-known for his formal garden where hedges of laurels and hollies were formed into grottoes, caves and arbours.

The vicarage, of brick with rendered walls, was repaired and much enlarged in 1824 at a cost of £600 following the arrival of the Rev William Buckle. In the 1841 Census his son, who succeeded him, is shown as living there with his wife, 8 children, 5 servants and a labourer. The vicarage was again repaired and enlarged at a cost of £500 in 1856 and enlarged again by the Rev Edward V. Buckle in 1879. It eventually had three storeys and nine bedrooms.

However by the 1930s its size and condition made it unsuitable for its purpose and in 1937 it was sold and demolished. A new vicarage was built in Garratts Lane, which in turn was sold off in 1973. The present more conveniently situated vicarage in Court Road was built in that year on land acquired earlier for a churchyard extension.

VICAR AND NEIGHBOUR

An early priest's income was not large, consisting of that part of the tithes not taken by the monastery and it was usual, as here, for it to be augmented by other activities such as farming. This evidently at one time caused friction between the vicar and his neighbour the lord of the manor.

In 1430 John Mathewe, the vicar, was fined for lopping trees in the hedge between the churchyard and the manor house without a licence and he was also fined for digging a deep and dangerous well on the lord's land. The following year he was again in trouble and fined for failing to repair the fence round the manor to the east of the churchyard. Later that year some of the vicar's oats were seized by the lord of the manor for non-payment of fines.

Any friction seems to have resolved itself later as the manor house ceased to be a royal residence and was evidently allowed to fall into ruin. When a survey of the manor was made in 1680 no mention was made of any buildings there.

15TH-18TH CENTURY

The external appearance of the church changed in the 15th century with the addition of new windows at both ends. These were an east window in the north chapel and a window of two lights in the south-west corner. This window was inserted following a bequest by the vicar John Woodcrofte in 1465 of funds for a "windowe in ye westende of ye chyrch behynde the south dore containing two "aies" (ie lights in a mullioned window). It was replaced in the "restoration" of the 1860s. The north aisle is believed to have been widened about 1465 and the north door renewed.

The chancel was repaired in 1631 and further large scale works to repair and "beautify" the church put in hand in 1716. This included extensive repointing, repairing and whitewashing of walls and the laying of stone on the floors, the repair of the roof and ceiling and the installation of 65 yards of wainscoting and associated woodwork. In addition the Royal Coat of Arms and 18 texts of scripture were painted in a frame on a chancel wall by the communion table. Other glazing, plumbing and painting work was also done at this time.

In 1750 repairs were carried out to the roof and plaster work. In 1773 the church was again repaired and whitewashed and the Ten Commandments painted in gold lettering by the communion table, which was said in 1841 to have been approached by four steps. It was evidently then that the lower part of the 15th century east windows to the chancel was removed and blocked up to accommodate changes to the church interior *(see figure 24)*.

THE STEEPLE

The first known reference to a steeple at Banstead was to steeple bells in 1549. In the late 17th century the spire was said by Aubrey to have been made of slates. It is known to have been reshingled in 1765 and again in 1783, when a 12 penny rate was raised to pay for this. The south and west sides of the steeple were repaired in 1788 but it still came in for some criticism.

In 1826 the church was said to have "a lofty spire cased in white tiles which can be seen for many miles around", but unfortunately from all points it was said to have "the singular appearance of being awry." Again in 1860 the spire was said to be "very much out of the perpendicular and not to have been otherwise within the memory of man."

In 1866 there is a reference to "the old church with its one-sided spire" at Banstead. In another account the spire is said to be "noticeably out of character and proportion with the rest of the building, being far too small for the church."

A local poet of the time, writing of Banstead, referred to

"Your quaint spire, by storm and ages riven,
Leaning, tired veteran, on the road to heaven".

The distortion and southward leaning of the spire, presumably caused by the use of unseasoned timber, was evidently remedied in the work on the steeple in

Figure 22. The church nave. *(A.W.A. 1842).*

Figure 23. The church nave. *(February 2007)*

Figure 24. The Chancel. *(Gideon Yates - 1826)*
 Reproduced by permission of London Borough of Lambeth, Archives Department.

Figure 25. The church interior looking west. *(Gideon Yates - 1826)*
 Reproduced by permission of London Borough of Lambeth, Archives Department.

Figure 26. The Chancel *(August 2006)*.

Figure 27. The church interior looking west. *(August 2006)*.

Figure 28. The magnificent 3 tiered pulpit. *(Edward Hassell 1830)*
Reproduced by permission of London Borough of Lambeth, Archives Department.

1872. Comparison of photographs of the church in 1864 and 1905 shows that between these years the lower part of the spire was straightened and strengthened. It is a broach wooden spire, covered with oak shingles and crowned with a cross and nowadays a gilded weathercock. The earliest known print of the church, by Seago c.1724, shows a weather vane.

19TH CENTURY

In 1826 the widow of the last of the six Christopher Buckles had a memorial tablet inserted in the outside wall of the north-east corner of the church. This commemorated the Buckle family, members of which had been buried in the family vault underneath from 1642-1821. At the time this caused offence to other members of the family, which had hitherto kept to a long tradition of very simple funerals and no ostentatious memorials.

In 1820 a new room with a fireplace and chimney was added at the western end for vestry meetings, previously held in a gallery in the church tower. Contemporary paintings showing a stovepipe in the chancel indicate that a heating system in the church itself was installed between 1826 and 1830.

More work was needed in 1837 with the rebuilding of the south chapel and the addition of buttresses to strengthen the walls of the vestry room. The vestry continued to meet there until 1870 when it moved to a newly built village school in the High Street.

THE CHURCH PRE-"RESTORATION"

How the church looked before the restoration of the 1860s is known to us from several interesting paintings of the early 19th century. Of particular interest are four water colours by Gideon Yates dated 1826 and five by Edward Hassell in 1830. Together they give a comprehensive picture of the church not apparent in surviving documentary records.

PAINTINGS BY YATES

The Yates paintings, two of the exterior and two of the interior, give a good overall picture of the church and complement one another. The view of the exterior from the west *(figure 9)* shows a large doorway in the tower, hitherto unknown. A view of the interior looking west *(figure 19)* shows an organ loft and a communicating door between the tower and the nave. The church accounts for 1716 include payments for "painteing ye 4 doores", presumably the three external doors and the internal door from the nave to the tower.

Below the organ loft are what seem to be the "18 texts of scripture writing" painted in 1716 in the "beautifying" work of that year. The panelling that caught the eye of Edward Hassell in 1830 *(figure 29)* probably dates from this time, as does also the elaborate carving on the three decker pulpit *(figure 28)*.

Reredos

The Yates painting of the chancel and the interior looking east in 1826 shows what C.J. Swete described in 1860 as a "handsome altarpiece of carved oak". It was evidently here that in 1773, as shown in the church accounts, "the Ten Commandments were painted in golden letters by the communion table at the sole expense of the Impropriator, Christopher Buckle."

It must have been at this time that the structural change to the east chancel window took place in order to accommodate the altarpiece. Yates's 1826 painting of the exterior and the photograph of about 1866 both show that the lower part of the 15th century window was removed and replaced by rather unsightly brickwork, spoiling the external appearance of this end of the church.

This in itself may have been one of the reasons for the demand for "restoration" and change to the church in the 1860s. At the same time the influence of the Gothic Revival movement and the commissioning of the medievalist, George E. Street, to restore the south aisle and tower in 1861 may also have been a considerable factor.

Paintings by Hassell

The paintings by Edward Hassell of 1830, one of the exterior and four of the interior, are also of great interest. The view of the exterior from the south in that year *(figure 20)* shows a hitherto unsuspected skylight over the south aisle. It is clear from this and other paintings that the church had been very well lit internally. This was completely changed by the "restoration" and not remedied until a clerestory was added to the church roof in 1898.

The lightness inside the church is well illustrated by Hassell's picture of the pulpit, which shows shadows cast by the sun shining through the skylight and the old south window seen in the background. Shadows in the nave cast by the sun are also to be seen in the painting on millboard of a family group by "A.W.A." dated 1842, owned by the church.

The latter painting also shows that between 1830 and 1842 the elaborately carved three decker pulpit had been replaced by one of more usual shape, although the sounding board above it was kept. This pulpit was itself sold and replaced in the "restoration" in 1867.

The 1842 painting also shows resting against the wall a thatcher's rake or fire hook, part of the village's firefighting equipment kept in the church. The rake was for the difficult and dangerous task of pulling thatch from burning buildings. The need for this may have arisen from an arson attack which destroyed two hayricks belonging to the vicar in 1834.

Figure 29. Panels in All Saints' Church. *(Edward Hassell - 1830)*
Reproduced by permission of London Borough of Lambeth, Archives Department.

Figure 31. The font. *(Edward Hassell 1830)*
Reproduced by permission of London Borough of Lambeth, Archives Department.

Figure 30. The font *(April 2007)*

Figure 32. John the Baptist - Detail from the Rossetti Window. *(February 2007)*

Figure 33. Ezekiel - Detail from the Rossetti Window. *(February 2007)*

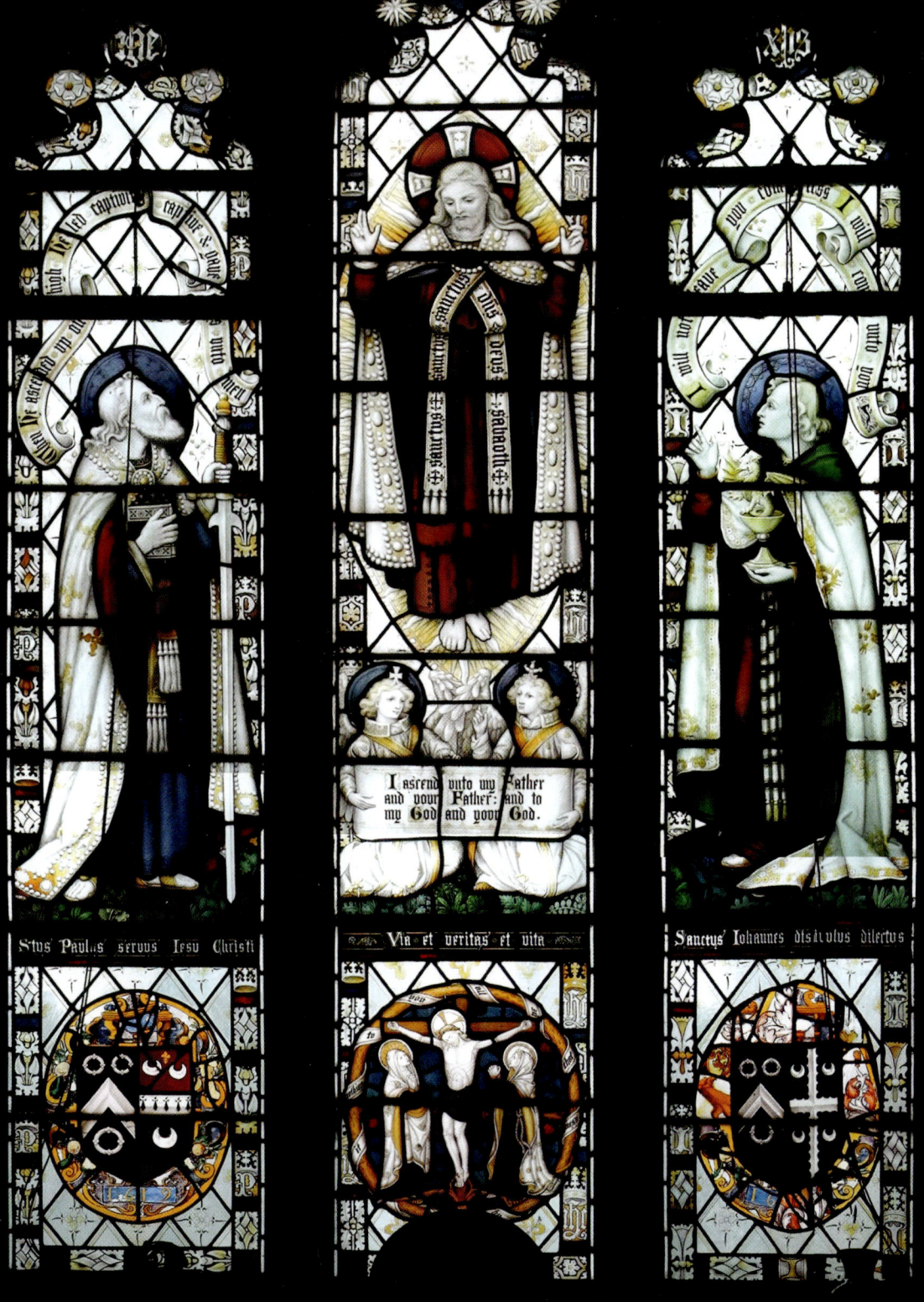

Figure 34. The Buckle Memorial window. *(August 2006)*

Figure 35. The present day organ. The pipes are for decoration only since the organ is electronic. *(August 2006).*

Figure 36. Facing west, the arcade between the nave and south chapel. *(February 2007)*

Font

The font with its octagonal bowl is dated c.1320-1350 and has a relatively modern round stem and base. The painting by Hassell in 1830 *(figure 31)*, shows the font with a protective wooden cover. This would probably have been secured by a padlock and be necessary because the font, containing holy water but standing in unconsecrated ground, was sometimes subject to vandalism and misuse.

By the time of the 1842 painting by "A.W.A." it is seen that the cover has been extended to protect the whole of the font including the stem and base. However the cover of the base was itself removed in the 1867 restoration.

Seating

As well as praising the carved oak altar-piece in 1860, C. J. Swete also observed that "the old carved oak pews are very curious". These box pews with their doors to keep out draughts are shown in both interiors by Yates and in the 1842 painting by "A.W.A.". Those on the northern side seem to be the best seats and would have been reserved for the families of the local gentry. At the time of the Census of Religious Worship of 1851 there were 142 appropriated seats and 118 which were free.

Figure 37. Only one volute is completed.

Oldest part of church

The oldest parts of the church are thought to be the arches of the nave arcades and the west arch of the north chapel, said some 100 years ago to show very distinct late 12th century diagonal tooling. The central pillars of the nave arcades are said to be a good example of Early English workmanship. These are octagonal columns on square bases, the capitals of which are moulded, each with four volutes.

It is noteworthy that only one of these volutes has been completed by the carving of a foliage design characteristic of the period on one of the south columns. One can only conclude that the craftsman involved was unable to complete the job. He may have died or it was found impossible to find the appropriate freemason or anyone else capable of finishing the work.

Consecration cross

It was also said that one of the consecration crosses could be traced just above the capital of an arcade on the chancel side. This no longer seems to be visible. Consecration crosses, small red-painted crosses each depicted within a circle, would have been incised in the stonework at a height of about 8 feet (2.4 metres), safe from defilement, and anointed by the bishop when he consecrated the church. A full set would have numbered 24, three on each of the inside walls and a similar number outside. They would have been easier to see 150 years ago when the walls were evidently of stone blocks, as shown in the 1842 painting by "A.W.A."

Church music

In 1465 the vicar John Woodcrofte made a number of bequests to the church including an antiphony containing the verses of psalms and money for "an honest priest to sing for my soul" and all Christian souls in the Church of Banstede for one year. In 1535 the will of Richard Waleys included the wish for a priest at Banstead to sing for his soul for one month.

Before the official recognition of hymn singing by the Church of England in 1820, the music in the church may mostly have been the singing of psalms and anthems, perhaps assisted by an organ. In 1751 a book published in London entitled "A Compleat Book of Psalmody, 2nd edition, set forth and corrected by James Evison" *(figure 16)*, included two psalms of local interest. These are a setting of Psalm No.135 entitled "The Banstead Tune, old version" and another called "The Borrough Tune, old version", a setting of Psalm No 128.

Both settings were presumably by someone closely connected with the church, perhaps John Edwards, vicar for 40 years from 1714 onwards. "Borrough" was of course the old spelling of Burgh. In the 14th and 15th centuries there was a Burgh church but all that remains nowadays is the name of the approach path alongside Nork Park, called Church Lane.

Church organ

By the end of the 15th century most parish churches possessed an organ and the above suggests that Banstead had one from quite early times. In 1644 an act of Parliament required the removal of organs from churches, the Puritans considering that instrumental music distracted the mind and soul from divine worship.

This resulted in many congregations in rural areas erecting west galleries to accommodate "choirs" of instrumentalists to lead the singing and this may have been the case in Banstead. However the restoration of the monarchy in 1660 resulted in a revival in organ building.

In 1806 the vestry minutes show payments for cleaning the organ and in

1809 there was said to have been an organ in the gallery in the tower. By 1841 the organ was said to have been removed but later there was a seraphine which, after an appeal for funds, was replaced in 1856 by a harmonium.

This served its turn until after a further appeal for funds it was sold in 1869 for £30 and replaced by a new organ costing £159. This was itself replaced in 1885 and repaired and resited in 1910. A new organ was installed above the tower arch in the belfry in 1919 and served until a new computerised organ was installed in 1979. This was itself replaced in 2002.

THE RESTORATION IN THE 1860S

The restoration work from 1861 onwards completely transformed the church. In that year the south aisle was rebuilt with funding from the family of the late Daniel Lambert of Well House and the seating increased to provide the church with a total accommodation for 350 persons.

The tower had been closed for many years but in 1862 its interior was restored with funds provided by John Lambert of Garratts Hall. The work consisted of removing the gallery used by the bellringers inside the tower, knocking through the wall between the tower and the nave, and extending the seating to part of the floor of the tower. It must have been also at this time that the west door was blocked off, so that access to the church was now by the north and south doors only.

Figure 38. The Rossetti window

THE ROSSETTI WINDOW

At the same time a new two-light stained glass window was inserted in the west wall of the tower. The composite design shows the prophet Ezekiel on the left in a green robe and John the Baptist on the right. It was the work of the Pre-Raphaelites Dante Gabriel Rossetti and William Morris respectively, with additional designs by Philip Webb. Both Morris and Webb trained under G.E. Street, the architect who had planned the work on the south aisle and church tower in 1861-62. The window was removed, taken to pieces, cleaned and restored by stained glass specialists in 1974.

These works in 1862 resulted in consideration being given to the needs of the church as a whole, perhaps prompted by Mr Street. It was agreed that extensive restoration was required. Among other things the nave and chancel were considered to be "much disfigured by high square pews occupying

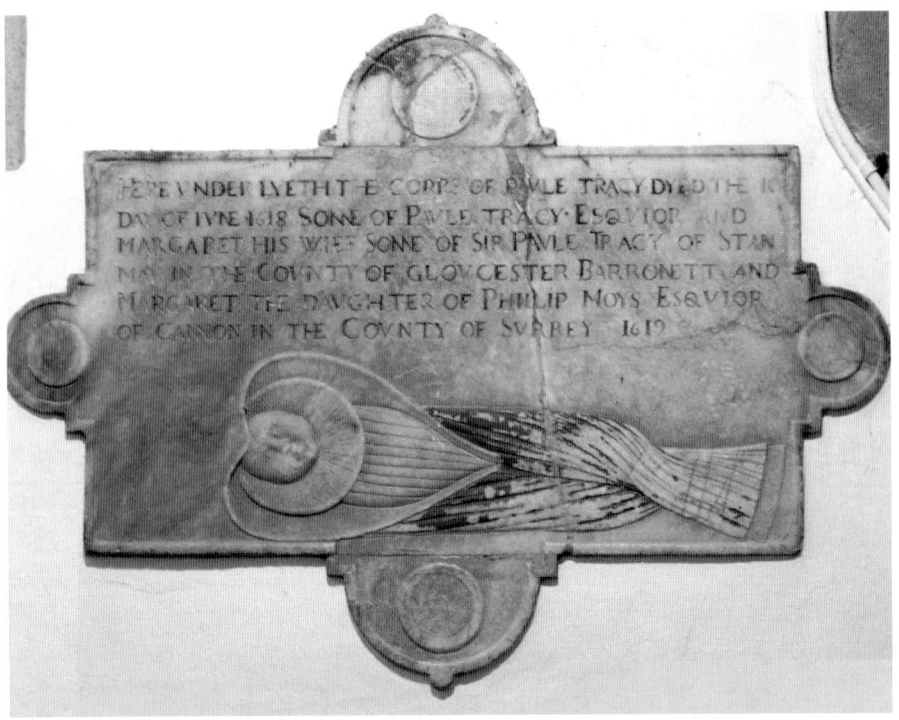

> HERE VNDER LYETH THE CORPS OF PAWLE TRACV DYED THE 10
> DAY OF JVNE 1618 SONNE OF PAWLE TRACY ESQVIOR AND
> MARGARET HIS WIEF SONNE OF SIR PAWLE TRACY OF STAN
> WAY IN THE COVNTY OF GLOVSTER BARRONETT AND
> MARGARET THE DAVGHTER OF PHILIP MOYS ESQVIOR
> OF CANNON IN THE COVNTY OF SVRREY 1619.

Figure 39. The memorial to Paul Tracy, the chrisom child..

an undue space". To remedy this the patron of the living, the 6th Earl of Egmont, agreed in 1864 to provide the funds to restore the chancel and chancel aisle, while an appeal to the public was made to fund the other works.

EFFECT OF RESTORATION

Mr Street was a celebrated architect, whose work included designing the Law Courts in the Strand. He was a deeply religious man holding High Church principles and considered that where church restoration was needed, it was a good working principle to restore it to the state it was around the year 1550. The works recommended for Banstead church were therefore very extensive, involving almost the whole of the church and including replacing all the windows and glass.

The church's appeal for funds said that the work required was very substantial but that both the church committee and the architect desired to preserve all old work and make no alterations that were not absolutely essential. The stated aim, in the words of the Banstead historian Sir Henry Lambert, cannot be said to have been achieved, but items of historical interest still remain.

The ancient carved oak box pews were replaced by open oak benches giving 100 extra sittings. The vestry fireplace and chimney were removed, together with the stove and chimney pipe in the nave, and new heating apparatus introduced.

The chancel floor was cemented over and paved with encaustic tiles. This raised it well above its original level, blocking out the bases of the Early English arcades and removing some other interesting historical features of the church interior. In addition the whole of the roof was retiled and three new windows installed to replace those on the north side of the church.

OTHER CHANGES TO INTERIOR

A chaste stone pulpit with a brass reading desk was introduced to replace the elaborately carved three-decker pulpit *(see figure 28)*. The old pulpit had incorporated the clerk's desk, a reading desk, and the pulpit itself, with a large sounding board above.

A Royal Coat of Arms, believed to have been that painted in 1716, was also removed along with most of the memorials. Those on the floor of the church were covered up, and the mural tablets were nearly all removed from their original location. Some were put up in the tower and others in the vestry, while some were never replaced and 30 years later were still lying in pieces in a shed in the churchyard.

MEMORIALS

One mural that survived is a small marble memorial to Paul Tracy. This baby, related to both the Buckle and the Moys families, patrons of the living, died in 1618 and was buried in his christening cloth. Another notable memorial is to Sir Daniel Lambert, Lord Mayor of London in 1741.

Before the restoration the church also contained many hatchments, but only one has survived. This is to the memory of Ruth, wife of George Brett and daughter of Edward Lambert, who died in 1647. There are still several other monuments to members of the Lambert family.

WINDOWS

In 1867 a memorial window to the Buckle family was inserted in the east wall of the north chapel by the Rev Edward V Buckle, who had succeeded his father in 1865 and remained vicar for the next 40 years. This window incorporates some original stained glass dated 1619 evidently taken from the hall of the family's ancestral home. This was Burgh House, the manor house of Great Burgh, which the Buckle family had vacated and sold earlier that century.

Manning and Bray, writing in 1809, said that this house was probably built by Christopher Buckle when he became the owner. This was in 1615. In the windows of the hall there were said to have lately been the arms of Buckle but they had been removed on altering the house. This would probably have been in 1800 when the Land Tax assessment on the house was increased from £106 to £140, after the 6th Christopher Buckle vacated the house.

C.J. Swete, writing in 1860, mentions that the east window had stained glass with the coat of arms of the Buckle family dated 1610. This date seems unlikely as there is no known connection between the Buckle family and Banstead before 1615, when the first Christopher Buckle purchased Great Burgh. His father Sir Cuthbert Buckle had been granted a coat of arms in 1579 but had lived in the City of London and been buried there in 1594.

With the building of the vestry in 1820 the 15th century 2-light plain glass window in the west wall became an internal window. It is now the oldest surviving window in the church and the only surviving pre-19th century window. It has been described as an excellent example of the best Perpendicular period tracery. The window of the south chancel was put up in 1879, that in the south aisle replaced by stained glass in 1880 and a stained glass window installed near the vestry in 1884.

Renewal of roof

The extensive changes to the church in the 1860s, with the removal of the skylight and the replacement of the windows, made it very dark inside. This was remedied in 1898-99 when the church was completely reroofed and six 3-light traceried dormer windows with leaded lights inserted over the nave arcade to form a clerestory.

These windows were copied from Compton church near Guildford which were much admired by the vicar. At the same time the stonework was repaired generally, drains re-laid and the interior decorated with stencilled frescoes. These frescoes were mostly obliterated when the interior walls were colour washed in 1919.

Figure 40. Compton church.

Church bells

The steeple has a peal of eight bells which over the years replaced the original five bells removed in 1553. The oldest of the present bells is Elizabethan, being the second largest, made by Robert Mot of Whitechapel in 1585. The second and third oldest are those made by William Carver in 1613 and Bryan Eldridge of Chertsey in 1638. The next, the tenor bell, being the heaviest and having the

Figure 41. The 3-light traceried dormer windows with leaded lights in the nave roof. *(February 2007).*

Figure 42. The Belfry. The inscription on the bell in the picture is: "William Carter Made Me" 1613. All the bells were recast with their original inscriptions by Gillet & Johnston (Croydon) Ltd. and rehung in an iron frame in 1921.

Figure 43. Christ in the home of his parents. A copy, by Miss M.W. Taylor, of the painting by L.E. Millais which hangs in the Tate Gallery, London. The copy was presented to the church by the artist in about 1950.

On a wooden hatchment emblazoned in colour. Arms: Argent, on a chevron azure, three bezants, for Brett, impaling, Gules, three narcissus flowers argent, for Lambert. The epitaph reads:

Here lyeth interred ye body of Ruth, Brett, the late wife of George Brett, citizen & Goldsmith of London & daughter of Mr Edward Lambert, of this Parish. Shee departed this lyfe the sixt day of November, A.D. 1647.

Behold the mirrovr of her sex and kind
Natvre adorned her frame virtve her mind
yet covld they not retaine her wasting breath
Nor free her from the fatall stroke of death
Her time is spent this splendid svnn is sett
In whose spirit all the graces mett
What good so ere in woman kind was fovnd
In this good woman richly did abovnd
Faith Hope and Charity her actions blest
Each in her sovle was a most welcome gvest
Life wrovght her death ove death to her brovght life
Svch was the fate of this rare virtvovs wife.

Figure 44. The one surviving wooden hatchment to the memory of Ruth, wife of George Brett and daughter of Edward Lambert, who died in 1647.

Figure 45. The orchard with the Church Institute and the Five Churches Open Door Coffee Shop. *(April 2007)*

Figure 46. The garden of remembrance on the former site of the Garton Memorial chapel which was badly damaged by a 1,000 lb high explosive bomb in 1940. *(August 2006)*.

Figure 47. The painting above the altar of the North Chapel. The three men adoring the child are past vicars of the church. From left to right they are: E.V. Buckle, William Lewis Buckle and William Buckle. *(February 2007)*.

Figure 49. The 1866 chest tomb of Sir Henry Muggeridge. *(August 2006)*.

Figure 48. Garton World War I memorial. *(August 2006)*.

The Bells of All Saints' Banstead, Surrey

Bell	Note	Weight CWT	QR	LB	Diameter	Cast	Inscription
Treble	E flat	50	0	0	28 5/8	1.2.1921	Warner 1892
2	D	5	0	19	29	11.2.1921	Warner 1892
3	C	5	2	16	31¼	26.1.1921	B.I Gloria in Excelcis 1638
4	B flat	6	3	0	33½	26.1.1921	William Carter made Me 1613
5	A flat	10	0	20	37¾	9.12.1925	Thos. Mears 1791 (Recast from No. 537 which broke in tower 1925)
6	G	10	0	0	39	25.2.1921	Robertus Mot Me Fecit 1585
7	F	14	3	3	44	1.2.1921	Lester & Pack Fecit 1756
Tenor	E flat	21	0	27	48 7/8	31.1.1921	Wm. Eldridge Made Me 1661 Peace On Earth Goodwill Toward Men

The Bells were recast with the original inscription by Gillet & Johnston (Croydon) and rehung on self-aligning ball bearings in an iron frame in 1921

Figure 50. Details of the Bells of All Saints Church.

deepest tone, was made by Eldridge's successor William Eldridge, described as "the great Sussex bell founder of Horsham".

The fifth oldest bell was made in 1756 by Lester & Pack of London, and the sixth oldest by Thomas Mears, late of that firm, in 1791, having been recast from earlier bells. The bells, the combined weight of which was about 4½ tons, were repaired in 1827 and again in 1872. The ring of eight bells was completed in 1892 by the gift by a parishioner of the treble (the smallest) and second bells, made by Warner, the repairers of the other bells 20 years earlier. They were recast and rehung on modern frames and bearings in 1919 and retuned and rehung in 1921.

The Banstead bells are well-known in the world of bellringing and have been used in BBC broadcasts. Pulling a bell correctly involves much skill. A bellringer at Banstead from 1928-84 and captain of the tower for many years, the late Harold Pitstow, was also for nearly 40 years a ringer at Westminster Abbey. For his work as secretary of the Westminster ringers and for services to bellringing he was awarded the OBE in 1977.

BELLRINGING

The poor state of the steeple commented on by early 19th century observers may have been due originally to the use of unseasoned timber or possibly later to neglect because of friction between the bellringers and the clergy. Bellringing had been discouraged during the time of the Commonwealth and it is known that by the 18th century the clergy had in some places virtually vacated the belfry.

In these places the ringers took every opportunity to ring, doing so mainly as a hobby and usually for gain. Hostility sometimes grew between the clergy and "ungodly" ringers, giving the clergy no enthusiasm to spend church funds on the maintenance of the bells or belfry.

In turn the bellringers sometimes felt that the clergy had no interest in bellringing and therefore no business in the tower. Attendance at church services was not necessarily considered part of a bellringer's duties. Furthermore it was thirsty work, usually requiring a barrel of beer for refreshment to be on tap in the ringing chamber, beer being the normal drink in those days. The church accounts for 1732-34 show payments of four shillings a day for "drink for ye Ringers for the four usuall Dayes of Ringing".

The reopening of the interior of the tower at Banstead in 1862 with the removal of the ringing chamber above and the restoration of the wall arch between the tower and nave meant that the bell ropes had to be lengthened accordingly. The ringers were now at ground level and in full view of the congregation.

We do not know of any hostility between ringers and clergy at Banstead, but the rules for bellringers laid down in the notice inside the church suggests that laying down the law may once have been considered necessary. The ringers met in 1893 to sign the new rules.

The Surrey Association of Change Ringers meeting there earlier that year had rung a memorable peal of 5,040 changes. A full peal of bells was rung all day in May 1900 when news was received of the relief of Mafeking, the ringers receiving £1 from the churchwardens for their trouble. A full peal was rung again two years later when peace was agreed in South Africa.

CHURCH CLOCK

A church clock was installed in 1931 with funds provided by Colonel T F Parkinson, a bellringer, in memory of his son, a naval lieutenant. The clock originally needed to be wound up every 3 days, with three weights at the base of the steeple, but automatic winding gear was installed in 1977, doing away with the need for this.

TWENTIETH CENTURY

A large King Edward VII Prayer Book specially printed and bound in a carved wooden cover was presented to the church in 1904 by a local celebrity actor, Edward S. Willard. Also in the church is a large copy of a painting by J E Millais entitled "Christ in the Home of His Parents", presented to the church by a local artist, Miss M.W. Taylor, about 1950.

Figure 51. The North Chapel known as the Lady Chapel which has links with the Buckle family. Note the panels beneath the windows which bear the names of Banstead men who fell in World War I. *(August 2006).*

Figure 52. The South Chapel is known as the Lambert Chapel because of its links with the Lambert family. The south wall has memorials to members of the Lambert family. *(August 2006).*

Figure 53. The Nave of the Church looking towards the Chancel (1905).

Figure 54. The Nave of the Church looking towards the Chancel (2006).

Figure 55. The North aisle looking west. Note the 15th century window above the wood panels containing the list of all the known vicars of All Saints' Church. *(2006)*

Figure 56. The tower arch and the south chapel. Note the great thickness of the tower arch *(2006)*.

In 1919 the north chapel was made into a memorial chapel to the local men who died in the Great War of 1914-18. In 1965 it was found that the roof timbers were in a dangerous state of decay and the whole building was re-roofed with seasoned oak beams and the steeple reshingled. In 1981 more repairs were found to be needed and the whole of the flooring renewed except in the two chapels.

More improvements and refurbishment on the interior was carried out in 2003. These included alterations to the vestry including the provision of washing and toilet facilities. The south-east chapel was converted into a vestry for the choir and at the same time the church heating system was renewed.

CHURCH INSTITUTE

A Church Institute was opened nearby in 1906 with funds provided by a brother of the vicar, the Rev Duncan Woodroffe. Until then the Village School had been the only premises available for the Church Sunday School or for activities such as meetings of the vestry. There was felt to be a great need in Banstead for a village hall as a centre of social life.

The Institute was built and fitted out and a working men's club inaugurated, its membership and activities being extended after a public meeting in 1914. Activities such as plays, dances, lectures, etc were provided for, with facilities for light refreshments.

Its popularity continued to increase and in 1926 after an appeal for funds it was enlarged with a new permanent stage and other accommodation. It was much in demand during the war of 1939-45 and afterwards, despite the opening of the Banstead Community Hall in 1975.

BANSTEAD FIVE CHURCHES

The Institute was upgraded and enlarged again in 1990 following energetic fund-raising for the admirable Banstead Five Churches ecumenical project in which a churchwarden, Councillor Bill Bryant, and his wife were very active. Celebrating its centenary in 2006 the Institute now incorporates a church office and the Five Churches Open Door coffee shop and lounge. This is run by volunteers from five local churches, pledged to work together towards harmony in worship and community service. A comprehensive booklet by Barbara Smith on the history of the Institute has recently been published.

CHURCHYARD

Writing in 1923 Sir Henry Lambert referred to the churchyard as being "now covered with stone monuments, which are, it must be said, for the most part no improvement on the turf graves and wooden crosses of earlier generations". Until fairly recently there were some interesting old wooden graveboards but none now survives.

Figure 57. The view of the churchyard from the south. *(August 2006)*.

There are several old chest tombs in the churchyard, of which two are Grade II listed. These are a rather dilapidated 18th century tomb of five members of the Wilmot family, about 20 yards south of the church, and the 1866 tomb of Sir Henry Muggeridge, about 20 yards west of the church.

With the great expansion of the village in the last 200 years, the churchyard needed to be enlarged several times, notably in 1861, 1904 and 1972. It now covers an area of some five acres, apart from the land forming "the orchard". It has now reached its full capacity as a graveyard and following an Order in Council of 2005, burials have now generally been discontinued. One consequence of this is that the maintenance of the churchyard is now the responsibility of the local borough council.

War memorial

South of the church is a memorial to the Banstead men who died in the Great War of 1914-18, giving their names and date of death. This was erected by the Garton family, once prominent in the district and in church affairs, who themselves lost two sons in the War. Amongst men of lesser rank listed in the memorial is a Brigadier-General, Archie S Buckle, killed in action on the Somme in 1916.

Garton Memorial Chapel

Featured in the churchyard at one time was the Garton Memorial Chapel of Rest, erected in 1936 south-west of the church. This was damaged in 1940 when a 1,000 lb high explosive bomb fell west of the tower, resulting in a crater 40 feet across and much damage to the graves there. The Chapel of Rest later had to be demolished and in its place is a garden of remembrance. A reminder of 1940 can still be discerned in front of the Institute in the form of the remains of an anti-invasion road block.

The history of the manor house

All Saints Church, Banstead — David Chance

The History of the Manor House

The earliest records of a manor of Banstead go back to the 7th century. There was a manor house in Banstead and all the evidence shows that it stood to the east and south of the church. It was very much associated with Hubert de Burgh, lord of the manor for 26 years from 1217 until his death in 1243.

Hubert de Burgh was a man of action and one of the King's closest counsellors and administrators. He was undoubtedly the most important historical figure to be associated with Banstead. It is not known how much time he spent here but Banstead is said to have been the favourite of his numerous manors. He certainly spent at least his last four years here after falling from favour in 1239.

His memory persisted for so many years that a tradition about the site of his manor house was still strong 450 years after his death. John Aubrey, the antiquary, wrote in the late 17th century:

"At the East End of the Church Yard, in a field, is a deep Pit sunk, said to be the Remains of the Cellars belonging to the Seat of Hubert de Burgh, Counsellor to King Henry III."

Writing in 1923 Sir Henry Lambert, the Banstead historian referred to "a depression in the ground of what is now Dr Caton's garden." With other evidence he thought it reasonably certain that this marked the cellars of Hubert de Burgh's manor house.

Dr Caton's house was De Burgh House on the corner of Avenue Road and Court Road. Even now the run of walls, which must be mediaeval, can be seen beneath the lawn in dry weather both here and by the neighbouring De Burgh Lodge. A cellar in the present Victorian building has an uncovered wall of stone blocks, possibly very old. A former owner, an architect, had a terrace built to the rear of the house covering over a well which he said was of Norman origin.

Twentieth century

A former air raid warden, the late Bernard Knibbs, remembered a bomb falling in 1940 in Dr Caton's garden behind the houses in Avenue Road and exposing an old cellar. He had himself later uncovered some fire-blackened flagstones some 3 feet down in part of his own garden in Court Road later sold for a churchyard extension. About 1970 a gravedigger severely jarred his arm in unexpectedly striking buried foundations in the churchyard.

In the preparatory work for the development of the nearby Cheviot Close in

1957 two old cellars were uncovered, evidently part of the manor buildings. A local archaeologist managed at the time to move enough rubble to gain entrance into a cellar. From there he got to a still lower cellar where he saw a "tunnel" with a blocked entrance. He had earlier met a lady who as a child had been in the cellars before they were blocked up but had been forbidden by her parents to play anywhere near them. Permission was asked to excavate the cellars but it was apparently refused by the local council. No trace of these cellars now remains.

As Sir Henry Lambert points out, the manor house would have been a rambling timber building with tiled roofs - all mediaeval houses were rambling, for they were not built to a plan and if you wanted more rooms, you just added them. This is borne out by the widely differing points around the church where mediaeval remains have been found.

On Hubert de Burgh's death in 1243 the property passed first to his widow Margaret, daughter of the King of Scotland, and then to his son John. In 1273 it was acquired by King Edward I, who entered into possession in 1275.

Royal Banstead

In May 1276 Ralph of Sandwich, the steward of Banstead and other royal manors, received a mandate to deliver the manors to Eleanor, the king's consort. It remained a royal residence at various times for over 100 years until October 1376, generally forming part of the queen's dowry.

Fortunately the fact that the manor belonged to the Crown means that some documentary records from 1275 onwards have survived. Our knowledge of the complex of manorial buildings is therefore not just based on guesswork and it is possible to some extent to visualise the manor house lived in by Edward I, Edward II and Edward III whenever they visited Banstead.

Edward I, one of the greatest English kings, is known to have visited Banstead in 1278, in April 1299, in May 1302 and June 1305. His son Edward II was here apparently in 1325 and 1326 and Edward III evidently visited Banstead in 1346, when four tuns of wine (some 840 gallons) were sent for his arrival.

As noted earlier the ordinary material for early building in Banstead was local timber. The framework of the house was of oak and the spaces between the walls filled with wattle and daub. This was sticks or laths plastered over with clay or loam, well mixed and held together with chopped straw and then painted with whiting made from locally produced powdered chalk.

It was a convenient and economical form of building but it had to be kept dry. As soon as the roof started to go and the rain got in, the walls of a timber building with wattle and daub quickly decayed. It is clear from the old royal accounts that this is what happened 700 years ago.

THE EXTENT OF THE MANOR HOUSE

The principal room in a mediaeval house was the hall. It was the common living room for the whole household with a raised dais at the end where the master and the more important members sat and dined. At the dais end of the hall it gradually became customary to put some other rooms of a more private character, although privacy does not seem to have been much prized in the Middle Ages.

The Banstead manor house buildings appear to have been situated in the area east and south of the church now occupied by the churchyard or neighbouring gardens. The records show that they consisted of a hall with at one end a room for the King and a room for the Queen. At the other end was a room for the knights or guard and some other rooms. Nearby there was also a great barn and the stables. A little way off and connected by a covered way was a large kitchen which seems to have been on the site of the present vicarage.

The Queen also had a covered walk where she could walk in the dry. There was glass in the windows of the hall, indicating a standard of comfort, if not luxury, at a time when windows were mostly covered by shutters or canvas only.

BUILDING WORK

The royal accounts show that on being taken over by the king in 1275 the first works to be undertaken were in tiling the roof of the hall and the room at the end, presumably the lord's or king's room. 4,000 tiles were used, giving work for two tilers for 17 days. A number of mediaeval roofing tiles were uncovered in the 1973 excavation measuring 10 inches by 5½ inches with an overlap of 2 inches, giving some idea of the area to be tiled.

In the following year 1276 extensive works were put in hand for the arrival of the king, Edward I and his wife Eleanor of Castile, to their new manor. The hall, kitchen chambers "and other houses" were repaired, the kitchen was tiled and a roof made for the passage between the kitchen and the hall. The knights' room was repaired, shingled and plastered.

Timber was felled in the royal park, now Banstead Wood, and transported to the site for building a chamber for the queen and for a cloister. The cost of the carpentry and building work in erecting this chamber and cloister, paid for at piece rates, together with the cost of the tiles, was considerable. Further costs were incurred in sawing boards, making shingles and laths, buying nails for them and buying lime.

The rooms of the king, queen and the knights were whitewashed and painted with colours and glass windows put in the hall. Two years later a large new stable and a new well-house were erected. By the year 1325 there was also a granary, bakery, cattle shelter, pigsty and dovecote.

The buildings were reported as being in good repair under Margaret, the second wife of Edward I, who died in 1317 but after that Isabella, consort of

Edward II, is said to have repaired the roofs but allowed the walls to deteriorate. Philippa, queen of Edward III, who was assigned the manor in 1331, allowed the walls and buildings to become ruinous so that by 1336 the two main walls of the hall were threatening to collapse. Works were evidently put in hand to make the necessary repairs and more work undertaken in 1351 and 1354.

FURTHER WORK IN 1363
In 1363 further work was needed and a carpenter was hired to erect two porches on the south side of the hall. The walls of the porches were underpinned and plastered, and roof tiles and guttering added. A total of 4,000 tiles were laid on the porches and elsewhere, taking a tiler and his assistant 12 days to do. When an archaeological dig took place in 1973 some lead guttering, apparently distorted by fire, was among the items uncovered, suggesting that the porches built in 1363 were later destroyed in a fire.

More extensive carpentry and building work took place from July to November 1370 with large scale works between 1371 and 1376, its last year as a royal residence.

In 1371, 18 feet of white glass was supplied for fitting into eight iron window frames in the king's room and the following year large scale work was undertaken to roof the big hall and two rooms annexed to it. For this purpose 10,000 tiles were brought from Reigate and a further 10,500 tiles from Ashtead, each requiring one man to make 10 journeys to bring them to Banstead.

6,000 oak laths on which to lay the tiles were bought in Croydon together with over 44,000 nails of various sizes to secure them. Two crests of knights riding were purchased from a Cheam potter as ornament for the ends of the roof. (A fragment of one such finial was recovered among other pottery by a local archaeological group from a field near Nork Park in 1998.) In 1376 more repairs were needed, both to "an old chamber next to the hall", presumably the original lord's room, and also to the cloister built in 1276.

THE EXCAVATIONS IN 1973
In 1973 excavation work was hurriedly put in hand by the Nonsuch Antiquarian Society prior to the building of the new vicarage in Court Road. Although only a small area could be excavated in the time available, flint walls were uncovered and remains of a deep well. In the well were found, along with some fragments of 13th century cooking pots and glazed jugs, a number of bones of birds such as swans together with a 13th century arrowhead.

This suggests that the well was close to the kitchen and that the bones of delicacies for the royal table, some of them killed by archery such as deer from the park, found their way into it afterwards. The erection of a well house was one of the works known to have been put in hand in 1277.

Apart from the roofing tiles, other remains have been uncovered in the vicinity. About 1890 it was recorded that pieces of masonry and old coins had been found from time to time. In 1903 tiles measuring 13 by 8 inches (33 by 20 cms) coloured red with a blue line on them were found together with fragments of pottery and some stained glass which fell to pieces and turned white on being exposed to the light.

Also found then and indicating an imposing building was a portion of a capital of chalk stone carved in the shape of a fleur-de-lys. Large carved blocks of Merstham stone were found in 1903 and again in large numbers in 1973.

The churchyard, especially that to the east and south of the church, would be a fruitful source of archaeological research should the opportunity ever arise. Meanwhile those with imagination may like to visualise the scene 700 years ago when royalty and the highest in the land with their retinue of knights and servants gathered in and around the manor house and no doubt participated in the activities inside this ancient church, as countless other Banstead residents have done ever since.

The Known Vicars of All Saints, Banstead

All Saints Church, Banstead — David Chance

The Known Vicars of All Saints' Banstead

Vicar	Dates
Ranulph	- 1315
Nicholas de Habbourne	1316 - 1322
Thomas Beauner	1322 - 1326
William de Storteford	1326 - 1329
Rowland de Huntercombe	1329 - 1332
William de Coventre	1332 - 1334
Thomas de Stake	1334 - 1346
Thomas	1346 - 1349
Henry de Shutlingdon	1349 - 1350
William de Sandyacre	1350 - 1355
Thomas de Notyngham	1355 - 1361
Thomas Englisshe	1361 - 1363
John Madehurst	1363 - 1367
Walter de Groby	1367 - 1372
John Hendeman	1372 - 1379
Robert Brokshote	1379 - 1389
John Sydenale	1389 - 1397
William Holstrete	1397 - 1398
John Neel	1398 - 1401
John Digge	1401 - 1403
John Dountone	1403 - 1406
William Kyrkeby	1406 - 1408
Robert Stratton	1408 -
....	....
John Mathewe - was vicar in	1430 - 1431
....	....
John Morecok	1462 - 1465
John Woodcrofte	1462 - 1465
James Wynter	1465 - 1468
William Ayssheford	1468 - 1477
John Stanfeld	1477 -
....	....

Vicar	Dates
William Cutson	- 1537
Miles Braithwaite	1537 - 1554
John Moys	1554 - 1564
Richard Brownwend	1564 - 1604
Simon Harward	1604 - 1614.
....	....
Thomas Pope - was vicar in	1616
....	....
John Hampton	1623 - 1636
....	....
James Staynes	1651 - 1659
Samuel Hinde	1659 - 1663
Nathaniel Hinde	1663 - 1714
John Edwards	1714 - 1754
James Wagstaffe	1754 - 1789
John Eales Francis	1789 - 1822
William Buckle	1822 - 1831
William Lewis Buckle	1832 - 1865
Edward Valentine Buckle	1865 - 1905
Duncan Woodroffe	1905 - 1918
Arthur Wells Hopkinson	1918 - 1929
Frederick Norman Skene	1929 - 1954
Frederick Schofield	1954 - 1972
Thomas Stephen New	1972 - 1993
David Newton Chance	1993

Note that this list is not definitive and, with some research, additions could probably be made. The names for the earliest years are taken from the Bishops Registers which are in Latin, in old handwriting, abbreviated and difficult to decipher. The Registers for 1417-1447 and 1492-1506 are lost so that the names of the vicars for those years are not known. The surname of the incumbent from 1346-1349 is illegible.

The first known vicar, Ranulph, "labouring under great infirmity of body and an incurable disorder" gave up the custody of the church in August 1315 to Nicholas de Habbourne or Halibourne. The date of his institution is given elsewhere as "before 1282" but it seems very unlikely that anyone in that period would have been vicar for the 33 or more years implied.

The names as transcribed from the manuscripts tend to vary, especially before the invention of the printing press in England in 1477. In the abbreviated old Latin handwriting it is particularly difficult to distinguish between the letters i, n, u, m, and w. With no agreed spelling of the earliest names the choice for names here is somewhat subjective. For example the name of the vicar from 1403 to 1406 is variously given as Dountone, Dounton, Dointon and Doutton, while the incumbent from 1564 to 1604 is given as Brownwend, Browwend, Brownend, Brownwent and Brownewent.

The names of the vicars in the Civil War period from 1642-1649 are unknown or uncertain. Some further details of the vicars together with a list of incumbents at Burgh church from 1301 to 1414 are to be found in Manning and Bray, although these are not always accurate.

A licence for an oratory at Canons near Burgh Heath was granted in February 1318 and Thomas de Banstede was ordained as priest there the following June. He had previously been ordained sub-deacon in December 1316, with Edmund de Banstede as acolite, and promoted to deacon in March 1318.

MAIN SOURCES

History of Banstead, Vols. I and II	Sir Henry Lambert (1912,1931)
History of Banstead, Vols. I and II	Banstead History Research Group (2005)
Banstead, Three Lectures on its History	Sir Henry Lambert (1923)
Victoria County History of Surrey, Vols. I - III	(1902,1905,1911)
History of Surrey Vol. II (1809)	Rev. D. Manning & W. Bray
The Registers of Banstead	F A H Lambert (1896)
A Companion to the English Parish Church	Stephen Friar (1996)
Old Parish Churches and how to view them	N E Boyle (1969)
County Churches - Surrey	J E Morris (1910)
The Parish Church, Its Architecture and Antiquities	E A G Lamborn (1929)
Discovering Church Architecture	Mark Child (1976)
Discovering Churchyards	Mark Child (1987)
Church and Parish	J H Bettey (1987)
Church Builders of the Nineteenth Century	Basil F L Clarke (1938)
The Older Methods of Building in Banstead	Sir Henry Lambert (1934)
Guided by a Stone-Mason	Thomas Maude (1997)

Index

A
Advowson 15
Anglo Saxon Christians 2

B
Banstead Five Churches 51
Bellringing 45
Burgh House 39

C
Censuses 21
Changes to Church
  15th-18th century 23
  19th century 29
  Chancel floor 39
  Effect of restoration 38
  Oak box pews 39
  Pre-"restoration" 29
  Renewal of roof 40
  Restoration, in 1860s 37
  Royal Coat of Arms 39
  Steeple 24
  Stone pulpit 39
  Twentieth century 46
Church
  Buckle memorial window 39
  Church and manor 7
  Church bells 40
  Church clock 46
  Church steeple 14
  Consecration crosses 36
  Entrance 7
  Font 31, 35
  Harmonium 37
  Hatchments 39
  Memorials 39
  Nave 2, 6, 7, 25, 29, 30, 34, 35, 37, 39, 40, 41, 46, 48, 49
  Nave arcades 35
  North chapel 7, 8, 23, 35, 39, 44, 47, 51
  Oldest part of church 35
  Organ 29, 34, 36, 37
  Pulpit, carved three decker 39
  Rossetti window 37
  Seating 35
  Size of 7
  South chapel 29, 34, 47
  The orchard 5, 52
  Tower 13
  Walls and roof 6
  Windows 39
Church Institute 43, 51
Church music
  Church organ
  The Banstead Tune
Churchyard 51
Civil War 16
Compton church 40

D
Dissolution of Priory 15
Dissolution of Southwark Priory 15
Domesday Survey 1

E
Earliest church 2
Early church building 6

G
Garton Chapel 52

M
Manor house 2, 8, 23, 39, 54-58
  Dr Caton's garden 54
  Evidence for 54
  Excavations in 1973 57

N
Notable Persons
  Rossetti, Dante 37
  Archie S Buckle 52
  Bernard Knibbs 54
  Christopher Buckle 15
  Colonel T. F. Parkinson 1
  Harold Pitstow 45
  Hubert de Burgh 7, 13, 54
  Lambert, Daniel 37
  Lambert, John 37
  Morris, William 37
  Moys family 15
  Muggeridge, Henry 52
  Nigel de Mowbray 5, 13
  Robert Moys 15
  Swete 30, 35, 40
  Tirel de Maniers 5
  Wilmot family 52

O
Orchard 5

P
Painting by J E Millais 46
Paintings by Hassell 30
Paintings by Yates 29
Parish life 8
Parish records 16
  Parish register 17
Paul Tracy 38
Place of sanctuary 13
Pre-Christian tumulus 3
Priory of St Mary Overy 5

S
Site of church 5
Skenfrith 13, 14

V
Vicarage
  New vicarage 23
  Vicarage PB 12, 22, 23
Vicars of Banstead
  Edward V Buckle 39
  Edward V. Buckle 23
  First known ordination 15
  James Staynes 21
  John Edwards 21, 36
  John Mathewe 23
  John Sydenhale 15
  John Woodcrofte 15, 23, 36
  Nathaniel Hinde 23
  Nicholas de Habbourne 15
  Ranulph 15
  Samuel Hinde 21
  Thomas de Banstede
  William Buckle 16, 23
  William Cutson
  William Lewis Buckle 16

W
War memorial 52

Y
Yew trees, dating of 3